PRACTICAL CHANGE...VOL. 3

MY VIEW FROM HERE

another anthology from

 THE WORKING WARRIOR MOM
.COM

By Noelle Federico

FIRST EDITION

For information or permissions write:

Wonder Works Studio LLC
Publishing Division
401 Buck Hollow Road
Fairfax, VT 05454

Cover Design:
Pam Smith | Creative Pear Marketing
Formatting:
Michael Swaidner, Colchester, VT
Back Cover photo:
Tia Rooney Photography, VT

ISBN#   978-1-7359355-1-5

Dedication

To GOD who makes WAYS
where there are no ways...
always.

To the WARRIOR in all of us,
who keeps GOING
even when we'd rather not.
You are stronger than you think
and worth more
than you imagine...

THE WORKING
WARRIOR MOM

My View from Here...

In Fall of 2014, I drove from TN to VT to visit my family for Thanksgiving… at that time I had NO idea of the HUGE changes that were coming my way. At a restaurant in Concord, MA a Priest I had never seen before came up to me, introduced himself and said, "Noelle, remember this verse and everything will be OK." That verse has become my touchstone, I am sharing it with you:

**"But they that wait
upon the LORD
shall renew their strength;
they shall mount up
with wings as eagles;
they shall run, and not be weary;
and they shall walk and not faint."**

Isaiah 40:31
King James Version

from Practical Change Vol. 2 and worth repeating…

Table of Contents

Stand Steady in uncertainty… have courage

THE WORKING
WARRIOR MOM

My View from Here…

It's been a minute since last we met on a book page, October 2017 to be precise. That's when I wrote my note to you in Vol. 2 of Practical Change... and here we are five years later. It seems like all the time has passed and yet it seems like no time has passed. In these pages you will find writings from the past 5 years that are being published in a book format for the first time. You will see that I often reference 'The Coffee Chat Show' which is a live show that I do every Saturday morning on Facebook at 8:30am est, you can find more about that at www.theworkingwarriormom.com. The show has been going on for about 7 years now, feel free to join us.

If you are meeting me in these pages for the first time, you can flip to the last page and read my bio — you'll discover that I am a results strategist, leadership trainer and consultant with several full-time jobs. The Working Warrior Mom is my public persona created as my giveback project designed to help and inspire anyone that is interested in creating a life that they want rather than one they are settling for. I was a working single mother for 18 years, I did not get child support (my choice), I have at different times been knee deep in dysfunctional rivers, broke, bankrupt, and terrified ...I have walked through hell so many times that I have gotten all the t-shirts.

In addition, I have been studying and practicing success principles since I was 12 years old, this year I will be 54---so that's a long damn time. Those principles enabled me to keep rising and recreating myself and now my view from here looks a lot different than it used to.

My mission is to use everything that I learned to help lead people out of where they are and into where they

THE WORKING WARRIOR MOM

want to be. My tests have become my testimonies and The Working Warrior Mom is the brand that I use to help and inspire as many people as possible. We don't charge for the content that I put out, we give it away with the intention that you will use whatever you learn to help as many people as you can. The world can use more warriors and leaders.

75% of any profits made from the sale of this book will go to my non-profit A Generous Heart (www.agenerousheart.com) which funds young literacy programs through community libraries.

This book is designed to be read in any order you choose---my wish is that in these pages you will find just the messages that you require to inspire and lift you into new actions that help you create a future unlike the past.

I believe that you can do and be whatever you want if you are willing to do the work. That's the key---doing the work on yourself and doing it consistently.

Enjoy what you find in here and feel free to reach out to me at noelle@fortunatopartners.com or join us live on FB every Saturday morning at 8:30am est. Bring your notebook!

With Every Good Wish,

Noelle
Fairfax, VT
June 7, 2022

*Let's begin with some
sage life advice…*

Make the Bed!

The importance of good habits comes to mind after weeks of playing the effectiveness game, practicing good habits equals our kids picking them up and emulating them as well…so I have learned:)

When I was growing up my grandparents were really like my parents and my grandfather had a rule about making the bed, he was a Navy man who served in WW II. As a child and even as an adult we were not allowed downstairs to start the day unless our bed was made. Made to his satisfaction that is, which meant made neatly and not just pulling a comforter or bedspread up over the mess from the night before. Fluff the pillows, straighten the sheets, put the throw pillows back on, etc. MADE.

So, as you might imagine after years of training and trying to rebel against house rules…making my bed became an ingrained habit. To my amazement it has also becomes my son's habit, that kid does not leave the house until his bed is made up perfectly… every day, no matter what. This is something that he started making important on his own, we'll call this #winning for me!

THE WORKING
WARRIOR MOM

Now let's talk about what making the bed can contribute to you, a few years ago I saw a video that US Navy Admiral William McRaven did entitled, "If you want to change the world, start by making your bed"--- I will include the link at the end of this post. It is worth watching. In his video Admiral McRaven points out that if you make your bed it starts your day with one task that is complete and that gives you a sense of accomplishment to go on and conquer other tasks for the day. Very good point.

For me making the bed has always been about creating order and making a fresh start on the new day—as you know I am big on how you begin and end your days. When you end your day by walking into a room with a messy bed that takes away your energy (in my opinion) --- everyone likes to get into a fresh bed at the end of a long day.

It is the little things you do every day that contribute to a new reality, small changes done consistently over time net BIG results. Darren Hardy wrote a great book called, "The Compound Effect" that talks about how life changing alterations start from making daily, consistent changes.

Take a peek at the Admiral's video and if you aren't already doing so… **Make the Bed!**

https://www.youtube.com/watch?v=3sK3wJAxGfs

THE WORKING WARRIOR MOM

My View from Here...

Taking Inventory

On a recent episode of The Coffee Chat Show we talked about doing an inventory of the relationships and alliances in your life and whether or not they are serving you anymore. I mentioned being very aware of who contributes to you and who takes away from you---everybody that you encounter does one or the other---they either ADD to your life or they zap your energy.

When you make the decision that you want a different kind of life you must be willing to take the actions that will make that manifest in your reality, often times that means that we have to divest ourselves of some stuff...people, objects, behaviors. Anything that is no longer serving you must be left behind, otherwise you will be unable to move forward.

It takes great strength to realize what you need to let go of and even greater strength to actually DO IT. You cannot move into the future that you want for yourself by dragging along people and things from the past, not all people want to change. Some people are quite happy complaining about how things never change vs. actually taking ACTION to change them.

Change is uncomfortable, however being uncomfortable causes us to grow as human beings and if we are not growing, we are becoming complacent and inevitably declining...

Time to start LOOKING at who and what is around you and deciding what stays and what goes—clutter, old clothes, papers, behaviors, people who drain you, etc.

Time to CLEAN HOUSE – the first step in Practical Change is to take inventory and be willing to tell the truth to yourself about what is no longer working for you. This can be difficult as often people that we love are not committed to moving ahead in their lives and for us to move ahead we will have to change our associations with them. The hardest thing to do is step back from people that we love that are unwilling to help themselves—in those cases it's either 'us' or 'them'—as I always say, "there is a reason the airlines tell you to put your oxygen mask on first."

Do not be afraid to admit to yourself what is no longer working and don't be afraid to cut it loose—everything that you want is on the other side of you making these changes. It is time to make NEW beginnings and start surrounding yourself with the things that will support the life that you are creating.

Cleaning Out the Fridge...

Last Sunday on Coffee Chat I started to talk to you about how thoughts and habits that no longer serve you can be just as toxic as relationships and behaviors that no longer serve you. The issue is that a toxic thought is harder to see, it is not as obvious as the other stuff.

Thought patterns that no longer serve you are usually hidden deep beneath the surface, and we think so many thoughts in a day, who has time to do a forensic assessment of every thought?

Yet thoughts become patterns and when we do not clean out the stuff that is not working, we can't truly manifest NEW good that will stick around.

My best analogy for this is your refrigerator --- if you have hidden rotting food in the back of your refrigerator or in the drawers and you don't clean it out then the fresh food that you put in there will become contaminated. The rotting food will literally poison the fresh food.

It is like this with your thoughts, habits, relationships, behaviors, etc. --- if you don't clean out the old stuff that isn't working then it will contaminate the new good that you are trying to bring into your life.

Getting rid of toxic thought patterns and behaviors is hard---suffering the consequences of not getting rid of them is harder. Pick your hard.

Personally, I would rather choose what to work on than to let it choose me---life is meant for learning--- continuing to work on yourself is progress and no matter what progress is a good thing.

Most people stop working on themselves, or they never start and that is how they end up stuck in lives that they don't LOVE.

Let's NOT be those people—let's be the people that keep reinventing ourselves in better versions--- we are a lifelong project, time to embrace that concept.

Unstoppable — Practicing Relentless JOY

Unstoppable- impossible to stop
Relentless- constant, continuing.

Last Saturday on The Coffee Chat Show I told you to watch out for when 'monkey mind' started to try and sabotage your momentum…I warned you to stay vigilant and not let that stop you. We talked about 'doing the thing and getting the power' –knocking out the stuff that you have been neglecting to finish or have put off. Now I am going to remind you that 'monkey mind' is not the only thing that will try to get in your way when you are on a roll—the force of chaos itself will start throwing things in your path to try and deter you from your renewed power. Here is a real-life example from this morning…

Having promised you guys on Saturday

THE WORKING
WARRIOR MOM

that I would dive in and start finishing shit that I have been putting off, I made good on my promise and spent the weekend catching up on the Leadership Training modules, knocking out modules of another training program that I have been dragging on since last March and finishing one of the books that has been sitting half-read for 2 or 3 years now. Getting all that done filled me with huge amounts of energy and ideas to do and ac-complish even more---so I woke up this morn-ing ready to rock and roll, walked into my sitting/prayer room and was assaulted by EIGHT shit stains on the WHITE carpet from one of the cats who must have had it on their paws.... EIGHT stains---mind you this was all BEFORE my first espresso...

NOW — some people would have let that define and ruin their entire day, however being as well-trained as I am and understand-ing that my JOY comes from making it up – I just proceeded downstairs to get the Resolve and a rag and I sprayed and cleaned all the stains with the cats looking on as if they had nothing to do with my plight...

THEN — I went back downstairs and made espresso and truthfully burst out loud laughing because I, honest to God, saw how chaos was trying SO HARD to steal my joy and throw me off my game. I realized that when I get into 'beast mode' with my personal power and productivity, I am a force of nature and the catalyst to making a lot of good things happen for people--- the forces of chaos don't like that—they like it better when we leave things undone, when we feel fat and shitty about ourselves, when we complain, overeat, drink too much, spend days binge-watching Netflix, etc. — chaos feeds off of apathy and complacency.

It breeds there and manufactures illness, depression, fear, sadness, and a plethora of other things that are not helpful.

So let me remind you today that you must access your unstoppable nature and decide to practice RELENTLESS JOY for NO reason other than the choice is yours---EVERY DAY THE CHOICE IS YOURS!

Choose wisely--- remember your Universal attraction point is where your vibration is—so choosing JOY means more joy finds its way to you. If I can be happy cleaning up shit on a Monday morning before coffee—you can be happy wherever you are as well.

"When you change
the way
you look at things,
the things you
look at
change."

-*Wayne Dyer*

Your Mentality Creates Your Reality

Recently, on The Coffee Chat Show we were talking about how your mentality creates your reality, so let's talk about that some more.

Whatever you hold in your mind will eventually become the circumstance in which you live— this is a simple, universal fact. Thoughts that are held in your mind will go forward into manifestation and become your reality.

Meaning that if you are constantly focused on what is wrong and what isn't working then you will create more of that in your future and meaning that YOU have the power to bring forth a different REALITY by cleaning up your mentality.

You can quite literally "think" your way out of any seeming difficulty and "think" your way into a totally different life. This can only be done IF you are willing to do the work—it takes work to change your thinking, you have to be willing to think new things and think in new ways as well as 'fake it till you make it'.

THE WORKING
WARRIOR MOM

When you start to introduce new thoughts, your mind will tell you that you are crazy for making up statements that are not yet true—good thing you know better than to listen to your 'monkey mind'.

Waking up every morning and saying "every day in every way things are getting better and better for me now' may seem crazy especially when your present circumstances appear to be daunting...this is what I mean when I say 'fake it till you make it"—you have to start saying and thinking the NEW thoughts first—- the results come after—so you have to be willing to just begin no matter what you seem to be in the middle of...

The most important thing that I can teach you is that you can change anything if you can change your thinking about it—this is far easier to say than to do—-to do this—change your thinking requires constant replacement of thoughts—it is our habit to think about what is wrong, to complain, to think about what isn't working—

Cleaning up your mentality means that you have to be vigilant and consciously re-place every 'old' thought with a new one. You must train yourself to think and respond in a new way.

Most of us are living unconsciously when it comes to our thinking, we don't evaluate our thoughts, we simply have them and act accordingly—we don't take the time to see that our reality has become a reflection of what is in our heads. Instead, we remain reactive to circumstances, and we slog through our lives complaining about what is around us and how things are going. This really is insanity—acting like we are at effect of what is around us—instead of seeing that we are very much "at cause".

My goal is to have you get conscious— to SEE that you CAN change things in your life—to see that if you will just be willing to do some work on yourself and be disciplined in it you can CHANGE THE GAME.

So, let's get you to at least start seeing that your mentality creates your reality ...

TODAY HAVE:

- BIGGER Conversations

- Broader Thinking

- Bolder Decisions

Creating an Inner Peace...
(written 5 months into the pandemic)

On a Coffee Chat FB Live, I talked about keeping your peace...let's talk about what that means, how you find your 'peace' and how you can protect it. With everything that is happening both in our homes and in the world right now, it is extremely important that you figure out how to get yourself into a place of peace and be able to stay there. This is easier said than done and I am relearning it right along with you. These last few months have been a real lesson for me in how much I try to fix and solve everything for everyone often at my own expense.

I have been learning that it is no longer my job to solve all my son's problems (he just turned 19 last week) and that it isn't my job to fix or save my family members or my clients—people have to be able to learn their own lessons...by continually trying to solve everything for everyone around me I have literally exhausted myself to the point where I feel like a dish rag that has been thoroughly rung out on the daily right now.

Peace comes from being able to keep your inner equilibrium no matter what is going on around you...it means understanding what is yours to handle and what isn't and it means being able to 'listen' without feeling responsible to act. Those of you fellow 'fixers and savers' know exactly what I mean. We are only responsible to handle our own crap...we don't have to take on the issues all around us because when we do we lose our own inner peace, become more reactive and exhaust ourselves.

If you are a God person, I would tell you to practice letting go and letting God— for those of you that have trouble with the God stuff I would say learn to let go and trust that Life itself will take care of you and the circumstances around you. Remember that what we focus on we will create more of, so taking time to focus on positive outcomes goes a long way in creating inner peace.

As the days pass and I continue to be stuck here I become more and more aware of how I tend to take on everyone else's "stuff" as if it were my job to solve it— I 'kind of' knew this about myself, yet over the last two months I have become VERY much more aware of it...and it is not something that I want to continue...

I realize that I need to be protective of my peace— that the cost of not paying attention to that is exhaustion and the inability to create

anything new— I have found myself unmotivated to work on the new body of work for
entrepreneurs that I want to bring out as well
as unmotivated to make videos for the small
coaching group that I invited a few people to
participate in— when I started looking to see
WHY I couldn't seem to get out of my own
way, I realized that I was using all my energy
to try and make everybody else OK and
happy etc. during these crazy times—— NOT
MY JOB. I get it. I am working on letting GO
and being responsible for MY OWN SHIT.

I am working hard to stay focused on what
works for me. Inviting you to do the same—
take care of YOU.

Time for A Change

If you did not catch my FB Live this past Sunday morning (7-5-20) then I suggest that you go and watch it or listen to the podcast recording of it. It will give more power and meaning to this blog post---judging by the response the video is getting over the last several hours I would say that my topic choice hit home for a lot of you.

Let us start by defining "toxic":

Toxic is defined as - very bad, unpleasant, or harmful.

There comes a time in our lives when we need to start looking around and acknowledging what is stealing our aliveness--- most of us are so busy and so bogged down that we don't even look around to see why we have less energy, why we are eating too much, why we aren't taking care of ourselves---we just think "oh that's just my life" or "that's how it has to be"--- I am calling BULLSHIT on all of those excuses. The truth is if you are anything like me you have said yes far too many times when you really wanted to say NO or you have done something when you didn't want to because you did not want to deal with what came from not doing it.

We go along to get along A LOT of the time and we think that we are doing ourselves a favor by causing less headaches in the moment—however at close to 52 and after running many businesses and raising a kid for 19 years all on my own, I can honestly tell you that I am not sure we are doing ourselves a favor by not standing up and speaking our own truth even if people don't like it or want to hear it.

Every time that we shrink ourselves to suit someone else, we DULL our own edges and then before you know it we turn around and we have become some shadowy version of who we were. When we do that, we don't like ourselves much because a part of us knows that we are saying yes to avoid conflict or going along just to keep the peace etc.

Yes, there are times we when we will have to do things we don't want to do and times that we will have to suck it up---I get that. What I am mostly speaking about here and on the live this morning is how doing this can become a daily habit instead of just a "sometimes" occurrence.

The pain that we think we are saving ourselves from in the moment actually is nothing compared to the suffering that we cause ourselves by not speaking our truth and drawing lines in the sand when things are not acceptable to us.

I don't believe in regrets---however I do believe that there are things that I could have done better so far in my almost 52 years and one of the biggies is that I could have made clear boundaries instead of trying to keep everybody happy at the expense of my own self-worth. I am much better with it now; however, it is an active project for me—making sure that I am saying what really works for me and what doesn't.

The biggest place that this one catches us is with toxic family situations or toxic relationships—often in these situations it can cause so much temporary drama to speak our truth and stand up for ourselves...

The cost though for not doing it is your energy, your joy, your 'aliveness'---I am asking you this week to start looking into your life to see what is unacceptable, what isn't OK with you, what you have been putting up with to keep the peace. The first step is to bring it to consciousness and then start thinking about what needs to be done to shift it. It will not happen overnight, and it will be a process---however you cannot wait one more minute to start saying what is really so for you.

It is time that you mattered to you---it's time to see what is not working and it is time to do something about that.

It All Turns Out...

After Mom died and I had some time to think about why she ended up exiting about 20 years before she planned, I realized that I had learned a way of being from her that perhaps no longer serves me. I see that I have 2 speeds--- WARP and Crash...that is all I know, it is what she taught me, and I see that it is what I have in turn taught my son.

This is NOT good--- I have realized this over the last 10 days---realized that I need to start resting in the middle of my life so that I can actually LIVE it and not just go balls to the wall racing through it to do the next thing on my list.

When did I get so freaking hardcore about just pushing through and making it happen---when did I lose my ability to appreciate the small moments, when did I start making myself feel like shit if I wanted to be lazy for a day or a moment---when did I decide that everything had to be so freaking SERIOUS!?

Mom did that---for 75 years she pushed herself hardcore and ended up exiting this life far too soon as a result. She used to tell me that she did not know how to rest--- in her journal I found some entries where she says that she made a decision to be "a serious person" and to her that meant giving up her painting and drawing and to some extent her

THE WORKING WARRIOR MOM

joy to just buckle down and build a business, raise me and get the results.

I believe it was at that point that she cut her hair very short, and it stayed that way… she felt short hair would be taken more seriously. Granted she lived in a time where women had to work harder to be noticed in business--- 40 something years ago---so I suppose she felt that going at it hard was her only choice. That makes me sad---she was an incredible artist and all of that got left behind decades ago---I have two of her paintings in my house.

On an episode of The Coffee Chat Show I started talking to you about looking at things like a cycle instead of like a line with a beginning and an end--- I'm learning about how to relax and let go in the middle having certainty that it ALL turns out at the end of the story.

There was a FB post that I saw the other day written on October 17th by a woman in Ireland that is 107 years old---in essence she says "stop worrying so much, enjoy your life, it all works out"—she said she has lived through ALL kinds of things and ALL kinds of loss and she assured us all that everything turns out.

Everything has a season—sometimes it looks great and sometimes it looks like shit, the trick is to know that it will come around again—there was never a night that had no morning.

Imagine how your life would change on the daily if you woke up thinking, "it all turns out"--- I keep saying to everyone around here, "I read the last chapter, it all works out in the end" and I have been really living like that the last 10 days or so and it is changing me…I am not taking everything so fxxxing seriously--- I am learning to just take the days as they come and do the next thing in front of me.

I feel like for Mom's sake, yours and my own that I need to learn how to rest in the middle and keep sharing that process with you on the shows.

Appreciate the moments---that is all we have…

A Little Love…

There are three quotes I'd like to share with you that I have been thinking about today:

**"Love does not begin and end
the way we seem to think it does.
Love is a battle. Love is a war.
Love is a growing up."**
James Baldwin

**"Love is an ENDLESS act
of forgiveness."**
Peter Ustinov

**"All things that exist
in truth
exist forever."**
Marianne Williamson

Most people don't understand that in all their relationships they are the decisive element. We decide whether or not to be offended, to be loving, to be kind, to be vindictive, to be generous, to be forgiving... other people do what they do, and we decide how to react to that. The mainstream seems to teach us that love feels good and that it makes you sappy and happy all the time and if you are unhappy then you must be in a bad situation be it romantic or otherwise...and so we have created a culture of folks that walk away from jobs and friends and relationships when they stop feeling "happy"...

What if real love was REAL WORK? What if loving your job, your kids, your friends, your relationships, your house, your pets, your country, your neighbors meant working to recreate that happy, sappy feeling day after day?

If we thought or understood that loving is really an endless act of forgiving and giving, then wouldn't we change the way we think about it? Consider that the real purpose of us all being here together is for soul growth and not for personal gratification or indulgence of the senses...consider that perhaps it is your job to use your relationships with people to further humanity as a whole instead of just using them to see what you can get for yourself...

Imagine a culture in which people put other people before themselves as a practice instead of just once and awhile to prove that they are not small selfish clods of ailments and grievances.

So many people that I know spend SO MUCH time worrying about who they can be with and what they can get out of it...people always seem so amazed at the way that I take care of the people around me, they think me so generous...the truth is that I was taught early on that it isn't about me...it is about what I can do for whoever is around me...it is about serving humanity to make things better for everyone...if we all lived like that what a different place this would be.

I wish that people would think prior to just reacting...I have a good friend that is recently divorced and every time his ex-wife pushes a button, he reacts...he isn't about serving her, he is about what a XXXXX she is being...I have a news flash...she will never change...he will have to change. Those people in your life that you believe deserve whatever it is that you are serving up to them...they are not really the ones being harmed by your behavior—you are. Your angst, your anger, your hatred, your unkind words...all those things you feel are valid...all of that just comes back to create chaos in your own life...negativity breeds negativity—universal law—always true...

I realize that we are not all going to start running around being nice to everyone and handing out flowers in orange robes...and I have my moments where I express my own disgust for people, places and things, however I catch myself and I know better and I keep trying to do better...that is all I am suggesting, that we think, that we look to see how we can forward the action of things instead of killing them with our negative actions and words...

The first step to changing any behavior is to first recognize it—you can't hope to shift something that you can't even bring to consciousness...

"The Spirit of Success is working with me, and I am in all ways guided, prospered, and blessed."

Catherine Ponder

Notes, Ideas and Thoughts...

Notes, Ideas and Thoughts...

What Do You Believe?

On Sunday I talked about the fact that you cannot change thoughts and habits successfully until you examine the 'beliefs' that are under everything running your life. I equated it to having something rotting in the refrigerator that you can't see and how until you clean it out it will contaminate all the fresh food that you put in there.

The same is true about the conversations/beliefs underneath everything that are running your life and you are not even aware of them. Things such as:

"I'm not good enough"
"There is never enough money"
"I can't do it"
"I will never get ahead"
"I'm not worthy"
"What if I fail"

The beliefs that are the underlying scripts of our lives come from childhood—we either heard them or learned them or saw them being emulated and then we decided that is how things were and so we unconsciously adopted them. Then our lives took shape and we didn't even notice that we were living out the things we adopted as beliefs when we were little.

THE WORKING
WARRIOR MOM

To change thoughts, behaviors and actions without digging down and discovering these beliefs really is like putting fresh food into a rotting fridge—everything will become contaminated and nothing new will happen. The OLD, OUTDATED, GRUBBY scripts will literally kill off the NEW good that you are working so hard to create.

So, when I talk to you about changing the game and changing your life, I have to first make you aware that there are scripts underneath everything that you have to find. Whatever they are they are OLD NEWS, and they are not the truth about you, in fact they NEVER were the truth about you...

When I was with you on The Coffee Chat Show, I talked about how my poor, pathetic scores on the effectiveness game had led me to start thinking that I must have some unrecognized, self-sabotaging belief that is still running me---I am still looking for it –hopefully soon I will have something to share about what I have discovered.

Meanwhile I want you to start thinking about what those beliefs are for you—the conversations that are running you, hidden under everything. We have to find those so that we can clean them out...

Remember that anything can be shifted, first it has to be seen...once we know what we are dealing with we can annihilate it and move forward.

Drawing Lines
In the Sand...

Continuing our discussion about stopping unhealthy situations in your life, let's talk about what happens when you start drawing lines in the sand with dysfunctional/toxic relationships...

First, the other people often don't like it and they get angry, belligerent, mean and/or distant...that's OK, let them. Second, your new behavior might feel weird to you...you may feel guilty or wrong or like you are a bad person...that's OK too...beginning to practice healthy behavior in relationships that have long been dysfunctional often feels "off". New behavior is an ADJUSTMENT.

When we are chronic fixers, savers and rescuers finally drawing lines in the sand and saying "NO MORE" feels like putting on your clothes backwards...it just seems "wrong"— you have to have space for that, if you can't wade through the discomfort while standing your ground you will never be able to make a lasting behavioral change.

Change is HARD, changing behaviors that no longer serve you is even harder—-especially when it involves close or family relationships. You have got to be willing to work through the HARD.

The alternative is to continue to participate in things that are toxic to you and the price for that is your vitality and your aliveness...my lifetime best friend said to me today, "you can't help another breathe if you suffocate first." TRUTH. There is a reason that on an airplane they tell you to secure your oxygen mask FIRST— because you are of no use to help anyone if you cannot BREATHE.

Begin to PAY ATTENTION to what is taking your energy and if that is worth it to you. I am so over trying to help people that don't want to help themselves—honestly if people don't want to do the work on themselves to be functional and healthy we cannot correct that and we certainly cannot save or fix them.

The price for behaviors and habits is the amount of life that you are willing to exchange for them. If something or someone is taking your energy and not giving anything back that is too high of a price to pay. You have to learn to make yourself important and make taking time for yourself important.

You are the only one that knows what works for you. Start drawing your lines in the sand about what you will tolerate and what you will not—-you don't have to justify that to anybody and it is OK if people don't understand — they don't have to.

It has taken me almost 52 years to see that I don't have to do things to please other people, that it is OK to say NO, that it doesn't matter what people think of me, that I can't save people from themselves and that the only thing I can control is my own behavior. Don't wait 52 years to stop over-doing and over-functioning— start drawing your lines now and start making yourself a priority.

THE WORKING
WARRIOR MOM

Clean Slates, Small Tweaks and Fresh Perspectives...

Spring is almost here and it's a great time to think about cleaning up, throwing things away and creating some fresh ways to look at your life. Wayne Dyer has a quote, "when you change the way you look at things, the things you look at change."

Most times we wait for things, people, and circumstances to change—we tell ourselves that we will be happy when something changes. The truth is that we could be happy RIGHT NOW, we could decide to BE the change instead of waiting for the change to appear in front of us.

The other truth is that most people don't want to be responsible for their own lives and what occurs in them. It is much easier to blame someone or something else for our life not being the way that we wish it was.

Creating a fresh perspective means being willing to look at your life in a different way and to be willing to see things that you have not seen before—things such as what is no longer serving you or what behaviors are no longer working for you. Telling the truth to ourselves about what requires change paves the way for us to create a plan of consistent small tweaks designed to orchestrate large changes over time.

Perfection in life is a myth, life is truly a work in progress and the JOY comes from embracing

THE WORKING WARRIOR MOM

43

My View from Here...

each moment and being grateful for however we are IN that moment. The "progress" part really amounts to a series of small tweaks on a consistent basis—not an abundance of huge, earth-shattering changes.

Often, we do ourselves a disservice when we try and make monumental changes all at once. That's a BIG job and when we inevitably fail, we use it as an excuse to stay stuck and as an excuse for no further attempts to change.

I've been thinking lately that small tweaks are really the way to go, one step at a time and when our old habits try and pull us back into the familiar patterns, we just make a small tweak to get ourselves back on track.

A series of small tweaks can result in a great list of accomplishments as you keep renewing things and tweaking behaviors this way and that to get the desired results.

Within this context when you have a 'bad day' and your goal isn't reached you can make some small tweaks and do better tomorrow.
The process of tweaking leaves a lot of room to improve, and it supports the work in progress that we are.

What small tweaks can you make this Spring that will bring you closer to the life that you want rather than the one you are settling for?

THE WORKING
WARRIOR MOM

Trust the Process...

In 2016 I had the idea that I should put out a yearly workbook to help you guys design a better new year...I worked on it a little, but it didn't materialize into form. Then starting in 2019, I completed the outline for that workbook which we now release annually in December.

It was a process, one that I could not really see because back in 2016 I thought it was a failed idea. God had more things to teach me before that workbook would be all it could be, I didn't know that then...I could not see.

Often, we are in the middle of a process that is bringing us to greater good yet in the middle it looks like a hot mess...it's hard, sad, confusing...we feel inept, like we failed, and we think that life is not working out for us the way that it should. We want instant gratification and quick results...at almost 54 I can promise you that anything worth anything does not come without doing the work to earn it.

Even though I know this and understand it, I still want everything to happen sooner rather than later, and patience is still something that I 'mostly' lack.

I never used to be good at the "trust the process" thing...people would say that, and it would make me angry...in my opinion the process should hurry up. That didn't do any good of course, things take as long as they take, and I saw that I could either learn to accept that and embrace it or I could just be aggravated all the time.

About 4 years ago I really started to learn the gift of trusting the process, by this time in my life I had seen enough things turning out well to know that if I was living my life right things ultimately would work out for me. To me trusting that life has a process means trusting that God is always working things out for the good and I can rarely see the whole plan at any given time.

That means that I must let go of my burning wish to control every freaking thing and TRUST that things are lining up and occurring the way that they are meant to. This also means understanding that my way is the inferior way...my will and my way are simply the means that my mind uses to try and control every thing...I have come to understand that there are a LOT of things that I cannot control and I have exhausted myself for almost 5 decades trying to make things bend to my will.

Not anymore, after the car incident in the Summer of 2018, I clearly came to see that there is very little that I can control—-HOW-EVER what was meant to harm me in all of that turned out to BLESS me—-every, single aspect of it. I learned so much from that reckoning. (For those of you that don't know, I was driving along minding my own business when a con-

THE WORKING
WARRIOR MOM

struction truck and trailer jumped their lane and came at me head on...I saw it coming and I was able to swerve and avoid a head on, however they completely sheared off the entire drivers side of my brand new car including the wheel...by the GRACE of God I was able to climb out my moonroof and I made a complete recovery, replaced the car, etc.) That incident taught me truly that I had no control over some things.

What I learned was really how to trust the process, at the time that all looked like a terrible mess and as I said it turned out to bless me in every way and really, truly changed the game for me——I learned so much about certain things—it was a process that in the middle I could not see——yet now years later I understand what God was doing.

That incident, moving back to VT and leaving my corporate job are all situations that have schooled me in "trusting the process" in ALL of those things I could not see to the end in the middle, in ALL of those situations I did not understand the entire plan—I had to step moment-by-moment trusting that everything was working as it should....and it WAS...

My message to you...TRUST THE PROCESS...you are being led where you are supposed to go even when you cannot see...in these situations you must walk by FAITH and not by sight. Keep breathing, keep moving...better things are coming.

Everyday in every way things are getting better and better.

Notes, Ideas and Thoughts...

Write a NEW story...

STOP Settling...

What are you putting up with that really isn't OK with you?

Where are you letting things pass by without saying that you find them unacceptable? In your job? Your relationship? With friends? With your kids? With your health? WHERE?

And the cost...have you considered that?

We are all settling for less than excellence somewhere, with something—-for me it's that damn daily list and the workout schedule— for some people it is their relationship or their job—every single person has some place that needs work. We settle because we tell ourselves that it is easier, we convince ourselves that it is too hard to make a change, that it will be too uncomfortable or too disruptive— that's bullshit— it is just what we tell ourselves to justify the fact that we are not willing to do what it takes to have it exactly the way we want it.

There are two solutions for this...

1. Stop accepting what is unacceptable, bite the bullet, speak your truth, make the

changes and deal with the consequences whatever they are. Whatever you have to face for speaking your truth has to be better then you waking up 10 years from now and saying "what the hell happened to my life?"

When you stay in things that are unacceptable to you, they steal your joy and aliveness every day and pretty soon you don't even recognize yourself anymore because you are so busy boxing yourself in to put up with shit that you can barely stomach—-yet people do it—-and they continue to do it....in the name of the 'kids' or 'bills to pay' or 'fear of being alone'—-bullshit excuses for giving away your aliveness....

Tell the TRUTH to yourself, whatever that is—-stop fooling yourself into thinking that you are operating in subpar conditions for the greater good—-at almost 54 years old, I say F**K that!!!

You are a warrior—-act like it. Period.

2. The second solution is to stop making

the current conditions shit—-stop complaining about them and being critical of them and start blessing them from right where you sit. You alone have the ability to change your reality—you can either do that by removing yourself from a situation or by being determined to bring blessing to the situation that you are in. You can never go wrong by blessing people and circumstances. You can also never go wrong by forcing yourself to come from a place of gratitude— if you change the way that you are looking at something or the way that you are holding it in mind, you will CHANGE the situation. It all starts with YOU.

YOU are the KEY to changing the game for yourself—-so it is time to either start shifting things and get out of stuff that isn't working OR start blessing those things and seeing the good in them. Either of these two solutions will bring you someplace NEW and that is where I want you to be some place new in your mind—-a place where you see that you can create the life that you want.

THE WORKING
WARRIOR MOM

Do The Work...

All of the 12 step programs have a saying, "the program works if you work it." This statement is true for many things including your ability to improve the quality of your life or more pointedly to 'change the game' for yourself. In my 52 years I have encountered a lot of people that were unhappy in their circumstances, yet when faced with ways out that required actually DOING something I saw that they would much rather stay complacent and keep complaining.

This is why so many people are stuck in lives that they aren't happy with...because they just want a magic solution that absolves them of having to DO ANY WORK. News Flash— there is no way to change without doing the work— anything worthwhile requires effort and change on your part. Period.

As you know the kid moved out a few weeks ago now and that has allowed me to actually pick my head up, take a breath and look around my life for the first time in many years—and what I see is that I created a magnificent life by using and practicing ALL the tools and principles that I talk with you about. I worked those things and made them a habit...and I still use them daily.

What I can PROMISE you with absolute certainty is that they WORK if you do the work. When Antonio was 18 months old I

THE WORKING
WARRIOR MOM

My View from Here...

had to file for bankruptcy— I was scared and broke, I had no car and I lived in a place that had mice running around it. I had known about all these principles since I was 12 and I practiced a lot of them daily—however after the bankruptcy I decided that I could do better, I decided that I would give it everything I had and I would see, if in fact, I could create a life and an income that I was proud of.

I did just that. It was and still is hard work—although it does get easier in time— the more you train your mind the easier it gets to be non-reactive and the quicker you can demonstrate circumstances that you want.

For those of you that don't know, I do not make an income from The Working Single Mom/ Working Warrior Mom brands—-in fact it costs me money every month— I do it because I know what it is like to be terrified and broke, I know what it feels like to be afraid that you can't pay the bills—I lived and worked with those fears most of the last 19 years—- I had no child support—it was just me and whatever I could create and earn. I created The Working Single Mom/ Working Warrior Mom brands as my public persona to help people, to give back, to coach and teach

THE WORKING
WARRIOR MOM

you that there is a way to create the life that you want. I am living, breathing proof that anything is possible if you are willing to do the work.

No matter what is going on for you today, hear me when I say to you that I am PROOF that you can create whatever you want. Believe this and then start to do the work to make it so.

Navigating the Unexpected

Nothing unseats us faster than things we don't expect—events, circumstances, or communications that we weren't planning for, these are the things that have the capability to throw you if you allow it.

These unexpected events can range from an unwelcome communication to some event concerning our job or children that wasn't in our master plan. When this stuff pops up the first thing that we want to do is REACT which usually includes a fair amount of emotion and that never really leads us to a good place...

Unexpected happenings are designed to challenge us and often we allow them to steal our joy and take away our peace of mind, we give into the panic, drama or worry and within minutes we are 'down the rabbit hole' and off into all the 'what if's'— this methodology is a recipe for disaster...

All seemingly unwelcome events come to teach us something and they come to PASS and not to stay—how fast they pass really depends on our response to them. We cannot control what comes our way, however we CAN control how we deal with it and how much of our energy we expend on it. I believe that everything has something to teach us and the faster we are open to the lesson the faster we can move out of the circumstance.

Our response to our lives is KEY, I often tell you that what we call a thing it becomes so if we start calling some circumstance horrid or a travesty or insurmountable then that is exactly what they will become. When things don't look the way you want them to you have two choices—one complain about them to anyone who will listen and lament about how horrible your plight is OR you can choose to know that somewhere in it there is good and you can start saying things like "I know what to do and I do it", "solutions present themselves to me", "Divine Order is present here and now" and my favorite "every day in every way things are getting better and better for me now".

Since I have been pushing that affirmation with you guys on The Coffee Chat Shows, I have started using it more myself. Today when my daily prayer partner asked me how I was on our morning call instead of listing out all my grievances I just said you know what "every day in every way things are getting better and better for me now" and they laughed and I laughed and said, "I could list out for you all my seeming problems today, however what the hell difference would it make?
So I am just going with this statement as

my answer— how I am today is better and better and I am sticking to that all day."

So far, so good and it is 12:34pm at the moment—- I mean shit what do I have to lose, right? I teach this stuff, it works, I tell you to do it—so instead of giving voice to my complaints I am doing it too.

It is all what we make of it—- if I list out all my crap then I only give it more power and I KNOW this for SURE. The best place that you can be is peaceful within yourself—no HIGH highs, no LOW lows—if you can remain at peace knowing that whatever is displaying itself to you is only temporary then you will achieve a level of self mastery that most people never see. It is a difficult thing to do and takes practice, yet do the work on yourself and you can get there. I still work on this myself regularly—-it gets easier to quell your reactions with time.

So for this week strive to keep yourself in a peaceful place and know that unwelcome circumstances don't come to stay, they come to pass.

THE WORKING
WARRIOR MOM

Pay Attention...

I was talking to one of my bff's yesterday, she called me to process her most recent breakup with a man that she had been dating for a few months. In the course of our discussion, we realized that there were some 'red flags' early on that she dismissed as well as some on-going red flags that she didn't give enough attention to. IF she had paid close attention from the start she may have saved them both time and energy as she would have admitted to herself that they were not well matched.

The conversation with her warranted me doing a blog post about PAYING ATTENTION...you will ALWAYS be warned when you are around someone that isn't good for you—whether it is a relationship or a friendship or a work association...if you are paying attention and looking at the facts in front of your face you will see the things you need to see. Sadly, most of us look through rose-colored glasses and dismiss important information in the name of wanting to create relationship.

It is important to keep in mind that nothing is more draining than a relationship that is toxic to you...relationships that contribute to you are life-giving...the toxic ones are energy stealers.

When evaluating someone to determine whether or not they are someone that you want in your world pay attention to a few important things:

- Watch what they DO---actions people watch actions

- See how they behave in public, how they treat clerks and waitstaff and other people standing in line etc

- Listen to what they talk about—do they constantly complain, are they whiners, do they speak from a victim mentality

- Look at their lives and what has happened to them, more importantly what KEEPS happening to them??? Do they have a long string of unwelcome events, are they always broke? Always blaming someone else? Always having 'bad luck'?

- Trust but VERIFY---- verify what you are told, check facts, check story details, make sure everything adds up

- Watch their habits---look for consistency...do they always oversleep, are they lazy, do they return calls and texts in a timely fashion, are they thoughtful, do they help, do they look to contribute or are they 'takers'

- Look at how they present themselves to

THE WORKING
WARRIOR MOM

the world...are they clean, neat or messy and disheveled --- is their car clean or is it a dumpster with wheels?

All of these things will tell you a lot about someone's character and they don't even have to say a word...people will mostly tell you what they think you want to hear...you have to look for what is being communicated without words.

Pay attention to the 'red flags' you see and tailor your behavior accordingly ---it will save you a lot of time and energy.

It doesn't matter how matter how you 'feel'— warriors GET UP, SHOW UP and don't give up... We don't let 'feelings' run us...

I'd Rather Not...

I'd rather NOT do anything today...I'd rather not go workout, write this blog post, have gotten up at 5:15am to keep my 'new' regime on track, I'd rather not have talked to clients this morning, cleaned up the kitchen dishes, unpacked the amazon boxes and folded the laundry that was in the living room...

I'd rather not figure out how to help the family members that are suffering from their own lack of discipline, I'd rather not keep helping my son figure out his life...I'D RATHER NOT.

However...I am wise enough to know that this is just a feeling that I am having, a passing thing, it is not who I am, it is not what I will do, it doesn't 'mean' anything....it's a feeling and my life is not run by my feelings... my life is run by my intentions and my promises...thank God for that.

If you have been reading my blogs or watching me on Sunday mornings you know that I have instituted a new habit of getting up at 5:15am and getting into the gym early---weekdays—in order to make sure that I get up, Tracy (who blogs for us and is my bff) and I have a quick call at 5:20am---I have news, we'd both rather not on most of the days. Yet we DO...we do it whether we 'feel' like it or not, we do it because we are pushing our-selves on purpose…we know that nothing new can be created by doing the same old things and we decided that we wanted to create amazing things for 2020. Our friendship spans over 30 years and we know that our word is all that matters, we know how to pro-duce the result no matter what, no matter how we feel in the moment or what we think. This is the stuff that keeps your edges sharp which I talked about in last week's blog.

Left to our own devices without 'checking' our behaviors or disciplining ourselves in un-comfortable ways we end up with dull edges…muddling along with things undone piling up all around us…how do you think that a hoarder becomes trapped by their own stuff…one box or pile at a time.

How does someone gain an extra 100 pounds???...one pound at a time.

Without checkpoints in our behavior we will go for the ways of least resistance…
"I will clean it tomorrow"
"I will workout tomorrow"
"I will fix it later"
"I'll deal with it when I feel like it"

These are the songs that we sing ourselves

THE WORKING
WARRIOR MOM

and then before you know it we turn around and things are out of hand and much harder to fix / change.

I was always told that in this life we will suffer because it is how we GROW and that I could either CHOOSE my suffering or the Universe would bestow it upon me. I would much rather CHOOSE my hard than have it foisted on me.

And so I do crazy shit like keep score on myself and get up early and force myself to workout etc etc...

Personally, I don't want my edges to dull and I am willing to do whatever it takes to create the reality that I want...are you?

Something worth thinking about.

Warrior Mom Training #101

Special Forces training in any branch of the Military is well-known as some of the toughest training and conditioning that exists...you must be optimally fit, quick to respond, ready for anything, tougher than nails, able to react in a split second and have the ability to solve problems instantaneously...you also must be able to endure physical pain, emotional discomfort and you must never, ever give up—there is no escape, no turning back, no "I don't want to"—you have a mission and you must complete it or die trying. Period.

If you have never enlisted in the Military yet you crave this kind of training for excellence you will be happy to know there is another way to receive it...become a single mother. I promise you that being a single mother will give you the training for excellence that you crave. The drill is similar to what I described above, however in this situation the training never stops—the classroom is your life and the lessons never ending...

When you are ultimately responsible for another human being there are a lot of behaviors that you can no longer entertain...there is no "I don't feel like it", no "I can't do it", no "someone else will take care of it", no "it's not my problem". You have TO DO EVERY-

THE WORKING
WARRIOR MOM

THING, it's all your problem and nobody cares if you "feel" like it or not...none of that even shows up on the screen.

No matter if you are sick, tired, lazy, angry, or sad you still have to take care of another human being...you have to see that they are clean, fed, safe, stable, happy and well-adjusted—even if you are not...

You are not allowed the grace of going to bed and pulling the covers over your head when life is looking shitty because someone is coming in your room, looking under the covers and asking you where their dinner is...

You may only have complete emotional meltdowns after your child is asleep and then you may only do it QUIETLY...there will be no crying loudly or howling in despair and it is really best if you lock yourself in the bathroom just in case the child awakens...not a good plan for your small person to see their beloved mother on her knees weeping in the living room—this could cause nightmares... and that just means you won't sleep either...

As a single mother whose ex-husband lived in another state, I enjoyed the fact that someone talked to me from 6am until approx. 9pm, on weekdays there was a reprieve caused by school, however on the weekends the talking was non-stop from sun-up to sundown(and now that he is 19 and has his own apartment there are TEXTS at all hours)...you may be filled with glee each Saturday and Sunday morning when you are joined in your bed by your son, Otter, Bunny, Kitty and Blue Covers...further enthralled when you are informed that you are TAKING UP TOO MUCH ROOM in your OWN bed.

There is no escape, no break, no quitting... there is only putting one foot in front of the other and doing the same thing over and over and over again...laundry, cleaning—constant cleaning, feeding, cooking, listening, explaining, yelling, crying, bathing, paying bills, working, taking care of the car, emptying trash, buying clothes, food shopping, changing shower heads and toilet seats, changing air filters, putting together toys, solving problems, teaching things, disciplining, etc, etc, etc

The list is endless...trust me. And all of it must be done with a cheerful heart because ultimately it is the path I chose. I chose not to live in a circumstance that was sucking the life out of me, I chose not to take child support or alimony because I wanted to move to another state and I wanted my ex to have travel money, I chose to raise this child as I saw fit and I chose not to give up who I was just to have someone to lean on...all of it my choice. My choice was difficult, it was a hard road to hoe...some days were much more difficult than others; however I have no regrets, not one...never have.

This training and situation is not for everyone—certainly not for the faint of heart...and sometimes it is scary, however you make it through. **TRUST ME—YOU DO.**

Like the Special Forces, the single mother must be ready for anything, able to act or react in a split second depending on the circumstance at hand. You must be physically tough and emotionally non-reactive, and you must be able to solve a wide variety of problems, some of them involving legos and superheroes. You must be able to endure picking up bugs and worms and must not run screaming when you see blood, you must carry Kleenex and anti-bacterial wipes and always have emergency snack foods in your car...band-aids too—you need band-aids.

The ultimate good news here is that this training will enable you to do ANYTHING... people are constantly asking me "how do you do all that you do?"— My answer...I JUST DO IT...If I stopped to think about how I can do what needs to be done, nothing would get accomplished...you just DO IT, it doesn't matter if you are tired, sick, overwhelmed, cranky, mad, sad...you just do it.

How I feel on any given day doesn't matter—no one else was there to run the companies, or get my son ready for camp, or pack lunch, or make breakfast, or drive to school... there was just me and I just DID it.

You have to create your life the way you want it, in every moment you have the choice to be enthusiastic or fowl, productive or lazy, angry or forgiving...there is no one else running your movie...it is just you, so make the best of it.

 THE WORKING WARRIOR MOM

My View from Here...

Choose FAITH Over Fear

Successfully Navigating Fear

I don't know about you but I am tired of fear and its seeming ability to steal my peace albeit temporarily...last week I had to do something that I did not really want to do, however I had no choice and fear was working overtime for at least several days...and every time it is time to travel fear starts its run at me...used to be that I was afraid all the time about money and not having enough of it, after 50 plus years I worked my way out of that and now fear comes calling for new things and quite frankly I am sick and tired of it--- I thought that you might be tired of fear too, so I thought we'd talk about it.

The New Oxford American Dictionary defines 'fear' as follows:

Fear- an unpleasant emotion caused by the belief that someone or something is dangerous, likely to cause pain, or a threat.

Here is what I LOVE about this particular definition, it says that fear is caused by a BELIEF that something is dangerous, harmful etc--- a BELIEF---- BINGO!!!

Herein lies the KEY for beating this shit--- it is a belief which means that we are giving it the power, we are allowing ourselves to 'believe' the thoughts that scare us—which ALSO means that we have the power to annihilate the fear. I talk to you all the time about changing the thoughts that circulate in your head, I am always saying that you first have to change your thinking before anything else will change…this remains true about getting rid of fear.

Last week when I was feeling like fear was getting the best of me, I picked one statement and I repeated it to myself over and over and over again until the chatter in my head ceased. Then I would be okay for a few hours and then the shitty, fearful thoughts would start up again and I would start my repetition process again. This literally went on for 48 hours--- by the way, as is almost always the case, my fears were unfounded and every thing turned out just fine.

Fear produces NOTHING that is good--- it simply steals your joy, makes you anxious, makes it hard to sleep, eat or breathe---makes you want to pull into yourself and not participate with others.

Fear is a thief and a disruptor and will always make you feel worse--- when we are enveloped in fear based thinking we are rendered unable to act—we are almost like a 'deer in headlights' because we cannot move to a place in our minds where solutions can find us---we are stuck and the thinking fear based thoughts keeps us more stuck….it is a

THE WORKING
WARRIOR MOM

vicious circle.

The way out of this is to control your thinking, you have to be vigilant about what thoughts you are allowing into your head and what the source of those thoughts are—you also must spend a fair amount of time talking about the good and focusing on thoughts and statements that will bring more good.

The quickest way to annihilate fear or anything you don't want more of is to STOP talking about it...stop giving any power or voice to the things you don't want to see more of---start focusing on your intentions and what IS working.
When we come from a place of peace things work out for us more quickly.

Start to really take a look at what causes your fear and where those thoughts are originating from---the first step in changing something is to become conscious of it.

Remember, you have the power here... don't forget that. Nothing can make you afraid unless you let it.

What puts the "Wonder" in the Woman?

I had a bad dream on Saturday night—It woke me up at 6am on Sunday and I was so unsettled that I just got up. In the dream Antonio was still little and my ex-husband had taken him for a visit, and I was freaking out because I was unable to reach them, and I was worried that he would not bring Antonio back. I woke up remembering the times that I felt like that, which were infrequent because the ex was pretty much not around the kid's whole life—that fact likely made me more concerned about trusting him when he did take the kid for a visit.

I had to remind myself that Antonio will be 20 in a few weeks and that he lives right down the street with his own phone and his own car etc.

When I settled myself with those facts, I started thinking about how nobody really helped me with raising him and then I thought about everything that I have been able to do for us—how I brought us from filing bankruptcy to where we are today—how he is going to be 20 soon which means that I have been at this parenting thing for two freaking DECADES.

Then I thought about how much I worried about shit that I couldn't control, about how f—ing terrified I was most of the time, about how many times I cried after he went to bed or when he was at school because I was just so damn scared about everything. I was on my own in TN for 12 years with him…his father visited once, my Mother visited never…that's another whole story for another day…

Point is that I made it, I did it— we are OK, we were OK, I figured it out, I kept going, I keep going. Now I worry less because I realize that it wastes my energy and when you worry you attract things to be worried about. None of us need that kind of help. Truly. STOP worrying.

These days I continue to practice what I teach you, vibe from a better, higher place, think the next best thought, elevate yourself on the daily. Appreciate what you have, keep doing the next thing and then the next.

Do me a favor—stop once in awhile in the middle and think about how FAR you have come, I never do that. I am trying to learn to do it more—mostly I just kept moving because I was afraid that if I stopped, I would not be able to pick myself back up—I did not give in to despair EVER because I imagined that if I did it would put me out and then who would take care of the kid…so for him I just kept doing the next thing.

I remember days that I was so afraid about money or something else that I could hardly breathe—so I would do the next thing and then say some affirmations or pick up a book that would help me direct my thoughts in a better way.

In case you ever wonder if I know what it feels like to be YOU, I DO. It's just that I am a bit further along and I created this work with The Working Single Mom brand to help you see that you can make it too—you can and you WILL. No matter what is happening now, you will get through it—I did, I do and you will.

Let me help you see what it looks like to get on the other side of hell—I will keep sharing my stories and you keep doing the next thing and use the tools that I am teaching—those tools and those prosperity principles saved my life and they work if you work them.

What puts the "Wonder" in Wonder Woman is you and the GRIT to keep going.

GRIT-

*courage and resolve;
strength of character*

THE WORKING
WARRIOR MOM

"What is grit?
Grit is refusing
to give up.
It's persistence.
It's making
your own luck."

Peter Diamandis

Keeping the Edges In...

On a recent episode of The Coffee Chat Show, you would have heard me talking about how we can avoid succumbing to apathy and complacency. I recounted a conversation that my son, Antonio and I had that morning...we have an immediate family member that no longer has their kick-ass and take names mentality and I was saying to Antonio that for all that particular person had taught me in my lifetime about keeping my edges tight and being effective, I was at a loss as to how they got to their current state. Antonio replied that he understood it and so I asked him to explain.

He went on to say that when you have things that you want to get done every day to feel effective and on purpose and then you miss the mark and have a bad day, it requires even more discipline to get back on the bus and once you don't get right back on the bus it becomes harder and harder to do so until all of a sudden you turn around one day and your life has very messy edges or no edges at all...

The kid is right you know...let's use my workouts as an example...I can be doing great, working out daily, getting it done, kicking ass and then I have an off day and I miss one. Then I feel like an asshole because I am off track and so maybe the next day I don't get it done either and then before you know it I have gone TWO weeks without a workout...

THE WORKING
WARRIOR MOM

and therein lies the story of the last 10 years of my life...pathetic in my opinion.

Soooooooooooooo kind of like the old adage about one step at a time, the question, "HOW DO YOU LOSE YOUR EDGE?" is aptly answered with one undone task at a time. After the live show I was talking to one of my coaching clients and I was telling him about the conversation from the show and he said, "yeah I get it. I still have not unpacked my suitcase from the trip in November, I have baskets of folded laundry laying around to put away and I have a collection of dirty silverware in my dishpan because I hate washing silverware, so I keep leaving it there and only wash the one fork at a time that I need (WHAT?!) (He lives alone in case you could not tell) and then I come home from work and just fall asleep on the sofa because I exhaust myself thinking about all the things that I am not getting done.

We laughed about it and he said, "I really get what you are saying about this, all these things are taking away my edge and making me less effective and they are such small things that I didn't even notice...yet when I put them all together in a list it is quite a bit."
And so it goes right? All of us have these little things, the messy corners, drawers, closets, cars...the things left not straightened when we go to bed because we will 'get it tomorrow', the laundry left unfolded or in baskets not put away because we 'don't have time'---all these little things dull us just a bit

every day—the too many cookies we ate, the workout we didn't do, the trash we didn't empty, the papers that we didn't throw away.

Years ago a Coach gave me an effectiveness assignment and I often invite the show audience to take up the practice with me …here is how it works:

Make a list of TEN DAILY things that you want to see yourself accomplish, ten things that if you did them every day you would feel like you were on top of your game. The items can be as simple or as complicated as you wish…brush your teeth, make the bed, take your vitamins, workout, read for an hour… whatever YOU wish.

Then make a checklist so that each day you can check off the task. At the end of each day give yourself a score, if you got 2 things done = 20%, if you got 8 things done = 80%--you get the idea.

Then at the end of each week look over the whole thing and give yourself a weekly average score--- data doesn't lie, this is a really great way to see just how effective you are being and also a great way to sharpen up your edges.

We created a free downloadable chart for this game—you can find that and other free tools at:
www.thecoffeechatshow.com
under the FREE STUFF tab.

THE WORKING
WARRIOR MOM

Impossible is not a fact, it's an opinion.
Muhammed Ali

Balance?! No such thing...

A few years ago I was featured in an interview about work-life balance for Moms and what that meant. I said then and I will say it again now, there is NO SUCH THING for those of us that are really living this life of raising kiddos. So PLEASE do yourself a favor and stop feeling bad trying to achieve something that does not exist. All these "experts" out there have all this advice about how to make you a balanced human and since in my opinion this is impossible to achieve all this stuff does is make you feel bad that you are so off point.

After almost 19 years of raising a human single-handedly, owning and working for companies and being solely responsible for the running of a home I can assure you that life is meant to be 'perfectly imperfect'. At no time during the last 19 years did I ever feel 'balanced' nor do I now:)

At the best of times it's a flow that moves along pretty smoothly and at the worst of times it feels incredibly overwhelming and like you are drowning in too many things to do. There is nothing wrong with you if you are feeling this way, this is honestly natural and a by-product of the lives that we are living. Just keep doing the next task in front of you whether that is a work task or a home

THE WORKING
WARRIOR MOM

task or a kid-based task—-whatever it is just complete it and move on to the next one. Don't beat yourself up because you had a work thing that made you miss a kid's game or you left dirty dishes in the sink etc.

You are truly doing the BEST that you can and you are doing GREAT...and never mind what anyone else thinks about it. Honesty, unless you have lived this life of single parenthood you have no idea...none. Also even if you are a parent with help juggling lots of things, there is no amazing balance to be achieved for you either. It makes me so angry when I read all these articles about how Mom's can achieve work-life balance...such horseshit.

So in the midst of the juggling act that is our lives what IS really important is that you figure out how to say NO to things that don't work for you and establish a system for taking care of yourself. Taking care of myself is still kind of a foreign concept...evidenced by the 25 hour bug from hell that I just had likely because I have been running myself in a million directions since the end of June.

Let's cover the saying NO part first—-you have got to learn to start saying NO to things that don't serve you or support you. The needy friends that steal your energy, the family members that stress you out, the work stuff that people are trying to overload you with and you are so nice you just keep saying yes...all that stuff is wearing you down whether you realize it or not. Saying NO is ok and even healthy, remember that if you go down from exhaustion or illness everything goes down so protect your time and your energy. It is important, your well-being is very important!

The taking care of yourself part you sort of have to figure out as you go, maybe its yoga, or a walk on the beach, a good novel, a movie night with friends, sitting quiet somewhere, a spa day, a regular workout, a weekly binge watching session on Netflix. Whatever gives you peace and some moments to yourself—maybe it's getting up an hour early to have an hour of power for yourself. Whatever it is you need to figure it out and commit to doing it.

Your health, your peace and your peace of mind are vital in this mix...in order to keep moving and to keep doing the next thing you must be in good shape, so you have to commit to self-care. By the way I always made fun of that statement in my mind...self-care...until I realized that I had to actually be the one concerned for my OWN well-being because it was nobody else's job. I have two speeds...go

THE WORKING
WARRIOR MOM

like a bat out of hell or crash and get sick for 2 days...pretty much that is all I know, at 51 I am learning a new way, learning that I can say NO, that I can go a little slower, that I can do what works for me....I am hoping that I can get you guys to avoid the errors that I made along the way.

Take the time to stop, breathe and appreciate the moments...they really do pass quicker than you think and inevitably you will look back and wish that you did something different. Let's try and make sure that you don't have too many regrets...appreciate how far you have come and take care of YOU.

It's a Flow,
Not a 'Balance'

Being the leader of your life requires you to be able to keep everything moving along at a productive and workable pace. The culture of the world might try and make you believe that you should be achieving something they like to call 'work – life balance'—if you are a well-functioning adult popular opinion says that you should be 'striving to achieve this'. I call BS and for those of you that have been following me since I started the brand in 2014 you know that I am ALWAYS calling BS on this idea. There is NO balance and there never will be, you are chasing after something that cannot exist for you and then when you can't get it you are upset and feel defeated and ineffective. STOP chasing after what isn't real.

Instead let's talk about what IS REAL— FLOW. Flow is a real thing; it means that there are times when you must go hard for a career/work thing and there are times when you need to go hard for a personal/family thing. At those times the other category will not get your full attention and that is OK. It is meant to be like that. The trick is figuring out the flow or balancing act that works for you.

Sometimes you will focus on one thing and

other times another, you may be on Zoom calls and then run to switch laundry over. Figure out what works for you and do that, stop trying to force yourself to live someone else's version of your life.

Also stop fooling yourself into thinking that 'multi-tasking' is doing you any favors---when you multi-task none of what you are doing gets YOUR FULL ATTENTION. Your attention is life-giving and the things and people in your life deserve your full attention. We are all guilty of 'half-listening' to a friend, child or partner while checking email or answering a text. Continuously telling ourselves that we must get everything done, we keep trying to do ALL the things at the same time. Then we make ourselves wrong for not achieving perfect 'work/life balance'.

Our time here on this planet is limited—we don't know when it will come to an end, yet we don't live like that. We act like we have all the time in the world to make up for missed moments—we don't.

Stop making the things and people in your life wait for your attention, stop telling yourself that after you are balanced you will pay more attention to your people. You are lying to yourself. You are racing like the hamster in the wheel and getting nowhere.

The laundry will still be there, the work project will still be there, the world will not end if you go color with your kiddo. LIVE in the moments people---stop pushing the moments aside with your quest for work/life balance and your multi-tasking nonsense.

Tis the season to BE—be with your people—be with people—give your time and attention, kind words, conversations—nobody cares about your busy schedule—they care about whether or not they matter to you. SHOW THEM. We are not here forever, let's enjoy the ride—REALLY ENJOY it.

I leave you with a quote from Gary Keller:
*"When you gamble
with your time,
you may be placing a bet
you can't cover. Even if you're sure
you can win, be careful
that you can live
with what you lose."*

"Don't give up.
Don't give in.
Wake up,
release your warrior,
and tell your
demons, 'Not today!
Let's dance
muther f--kers!'
Keep fighting
the good fight."

Helen Edwards
Nothing Sexier Than Freedom

Notes, Ideas and Thoughts...

Notes, Ideas and Thoughts...

Pain, No Gain...

"You will suffer one of two pains in your lifetime—the pain of disciplining yourself or the pain of regret from not disciplining yourself. That is a hard truth no matter what you think or what you want to believe."

"You must learn to go to war with yourself on certain character traits, habits and/or addictions or you will suffer from not doing so."

I have heard the above things many, many times over the last 50 plus years and NEVER did they sink in as much as they are right now. Now I am watching two people literally suffer horribly daily from NOT disciplining themselves when it was hard to do so.

Whatever they told themselves on a daily basis for decades that made it OK to not take care of their physical bodies and their health is not even close to worth what they are suffering now--- I promise you that it is IMPERATIVE that you take care of yourself--- eating right and doing something to exercise on a regular and consistent basis is worth every momentary pain that it might cause you now—to find the time or fit it in or force yourself to do it.

That drink that you don't have, the cupcakes that you don't eat, the ice cream you walk away from the cigarette you don't smoke---whatever it is get it under control NOW.

Do NOT wait until tomorrow, or next Tuesday or your next birthday or for the kids to be out of preschool or for the stress to be over---GET ON IT NOW.

Watching people that you care about live in hell on a daily basis will make you understand VERY quickly that the time to discipline yourself is RIGHT NOW. Our job in this life is to keep learning and keep pushing ourselves to do better and be better---whatever the hell that means for each of us.

Only YOU can say where you need to start shoring yourself up...and believe me you know where those places are and you know the stories that you are telling yourself about WHY you don't do what you need to do.

Physical health is something that I cannot stress enough--- if I showed you right now what I am having to witness you would weep—good people that were vibrant and bright lights diminished now to mere shadows of themselves due to extra weight, bad diets and the inability to get consistent exercise which leads to catastrophic outcomes with physical and mental well-being--- and ALL of this could have been prevented if they had chosen their hard instead of waiting for it to choose them.

There is nothing more heartbreaking than watching this and understanding that you cannot help or save people that will not help or save themselves---so what I CAN do is USE this to make a difference in my life and perhaps in yours too.

I force myself to do something at least 4 days a week -- at the very least yoga and on most days yoga and then a workout of some sort--- I want to be running up and down stairs easily when I am 80 plus---

PLEASE take care of yourselves--- start doing it now--- TODAY.

THE WORKING
WARRIOR MOM

What About You?

On an episode of The Coffee Chat Show we talked about making sure that you are taking time to take care of yourself, and I pointed out that you can't help someone else if you are not well. I reminded you all that there is a reason on an airplane they tell you to put your oxygen mask on first and then help others...a poignant way to illustrate my point.

The first thing that happens when you have a lot of toxic relationships or situations in your life is that you stop checking in with yourself about how YOU are because of course you are waaaayyyyy too busy caretaking and enabling to be worried about your own well-being.

In addition to drawing lines in the sand about what is acceptable to you and what isn't you also have to start looking at what you need to do for yourself that you are not doing. Can be as simple as taking 15 minutes for yourself everyday with no distractions or as complex as sticking to a daily workout schedule— only YOU can say what you need to function optimally.

Some of you may not even know the answer to the question, "what do I need?" —if that is the case then it's time to find out.

What do you require to feel centered and happy and peaceful?

Who do you need to start saying NO to?

What new habits do you need to acquire for taking better care of yourself?

What relationships are no longer serving you in their current format?

These are all valuable questions to start looking at. Often, we are so focused on just surviving that we forget it IS possible to thrive. You are of no value to anyone if you are not well or barely functioning...as a parent you have to take care of yourself first in order to do what you must do for the kiddos...this whole idea that you don't have time to take care of you is a bullshit construct that must be left behind.

Too many of us are over doing, overcompensating and enabling and it is costing us our health, our joy and our peace of mind...our survival and our ability to be vibrant and thriving is dependent upon us putting ourselves first.

I have news— nobody is coming to save you—- it is time that you saved yourself.
It is our responsibility to start speaking up and start taking the time that we require to get ourselves in order each day so that we can

THE WORKING
WARRIOR MOM

face things from a position of strength. Your mental and physical health are your most important assets — without them everything else becomes much more difficult if not impossible in some extreme cases.

Begin NOW—start looking at what you need and start carving out the time to make that happen— and start saying NO to the people and things that are stealing your energy and not giving anything back—- it's never too late to change the game.

We BEND, yet do not Break...

Reflections at 50...

In 25 days I turn 50. I decided that was worth talking to you about this morning...at the moment the self-loathing is at an all-time high because there are some things that are not the way I wanted them to be for my 50th birthday. It's been a hard year, in April 2017 I left the corporate world as most of you know and by doing so I cut my income by about 2/3 and my expenses stayed the same:)

My decision there was based on the fact that I wanted to work for myself again doing the things that I felt mattered or at least, perhaps helping to leave the world better than I found it. Although still happy with my decision the economic consequences have been a trial of their own, couple that with the fact that I intended to weigh ten pounds less than I currently do and you can begin to see how the self-loathing is making so much noise today...copious amounts of coffee is helping to dull the chatter...and of course writing to you guys always helps...

So, when one reflects on the first 50 years of their life they may ask themselves questions such as---what is the biggest misstep that I have made?

My answer to that is not understanding my worth, I have discovered over the last decade just how much havoc a low self-worth can wreak...let's embellish on that a bit...

THE WORKING
WARRIOR MOM

My View from Here...

Had I really possessed any self-worth when I was much younger I would have made every decision differently…growing up in an amazing yet highly dysfunctional family that drank way too much was not a recipe for developing a high self-worth quotient and in retrospect it clouded every, single move I made until I was in my mid-40's. If you don't value yourself you will accept things that you shouldn't, take actions that don't take care of YOU and make decisions to please and accommodate other people. You will also devalue yourself in the workplace and teach others to do the same because of course how can we expect anyone to treat us better than we treat ourselves?

Over time and especially within the last year I have come to understand at a much deeper level what it means to realize my own worth both as a woman and as a professional also as a human being. In the last year I have been surprised by people in good ways and in bad ways and I have learned so much.

Not being one for regrets and firmly believing that there are no mistakes, I am determined to face this birthday with GRACE and GRATITUDE… …the intention is, as always, that my experiences may somehow give you strength or shine a light on something that you need to see. All my tests become my testimony…

THE WORKING
WARRIOR MOM

51 Approaches!

When did my skin get so damn OLD looking??? These are the things that I am thinking as I look at last night's video...51 that is how old I will be in about a month, 51 years on the planet with an 18-year-old son.

18 years...where the hell did that GO??? 18 years of being a working single mom, 18 years of being solely responsible for every freaking thing—- how the hell did I even DO that???? Yet, here I sit...out the other side and in fact, I did do it and I did a pretty good job. The kid turned out pretty exceptional even in the face of my many shortcomings...

So what have I learned and what wisdom can I impart to help you through whatever stage of this adventure you are in?

Here we go...

• STOP worrying so much, it isn't helping anything. All it does is make you crazy and honest to God shit DOES work out. We hardly ever can see how, yet it does and you simply HAVE TO TRUST THAT IT WILL.

• Be honest with your kids, let them see you be REAL...acting like you are OK when you are NOT OK just screws them up because they can FEEL that you aren't right and you are usually all they have—-so let them see the warrior that you are, let them see that you can be afraid and do it anyway...let them see that you can not feel well and do it anyway...let them see what it is like to overcome things—it is only going to make them stronger, better adults.

• Kids KNOW, whatever it is that you think you are hiding from them, they already know—-so just be honest. Life is hard and we prevail, show them that—don't make them think that there won't be challenges—-show them what it is like to be real.

• Take care of yourself, if you go down there is no one to cover for you—-your health and your well-being are a PRIORITY. PERIOD.

• KNOW YOUR WORTH — I can't say this one enough...I made so many missteps over the years because I didn't understand my worth...don't do that. Don't settle, don't 'put up with shit'— know your worth.

• The kids are gonna be OK, they are going to make it. As long as you are doing your best and you are being authentic then they are going to be just fine...stop worrying.

• We are not perfect, we are not meant to be perfect—- we screw shit up, it's

THE WORKING
WARRIOR MOM

human nature—- just keep doing the best you can.

• Don't let fear stop you, have the fear and do it anyway—that's all there is— just keep going, doing the next thing in front of you.

• Help as MANY people as possible, always.

• Give back everywhere you can, be generous of Spirit—everyone is fighting their own battles that we know nothing about—be kind.

• Take the high road, it isn't crowded up there and don't sweat it, karma never loses an address—let the Universe handle the people that were less than kind to you, you have better things to do.

• Always keep learning, reading, pushing yourself—-as I said before don't settle—-keep pushing yourself, it's how you grow.

• Talk to your kids, listen to them— don't be so busy trying to survive that you forget to LIVE.

• Have GRACE for yourself and others—not everything has to be perfect all the time—cut yourself some slack...I am telling you it all works out at the end of the story...

• Acknowledge the small miracles and have gratitude for how far you have come, we often are so busy just trying to get through the day that we forget to give thanks for the progress—there is always something to be grateful for.

It's funny to be sitting in this place 18 plus years later, looking back on raising this boy on my own. At the beginning it seemed insurmountable, in the middle it was the hardest thing I have ever done, at the end it was the BEST training that I have ever had. I can produce results that nobody else can, I don't let anything stop me, I don't make excuses and my mantra has become "whatever it takes"—-I don't accept 'impossible' as a descriptor and I KNOW from walking through FIRE and HELL that you can and you WILL get through whatever you are facing.

You know me, I am always straight with you guys and this was the hardest thing that I have ever done, raising this child with no child support and being the sole source of everything that he required for 18 years plus:). However, it taught me skills and strengths that I would never have learned any other way and it built me into a warrior that now helps other people——that part is my greatest blessing.

Let my testimony become your inspiration—- if I could get out the other side successfully so will you...

THE WORKING
WARRIOR MOM

Here's to my approaching
51st birthday...
Let's see what God
has planned,
it's bound to be
an adventure and
you guys will be along
for the ride...

Fire Seasons...
the Viewpoint at 51

Tomorrow...51?!?! WTF? How did that even happen????

I was literally just, like 30! The kid is 18 now too, going on 60 or so he thinks...he's moving out soon, looking for an apartment with his friends as he works full time as a Sous Chef and tells me it isn't "cool" to be a Sous Chef and living at home....he says it is ruining his image....pardon me while I roll around on the floor laughing. I am ruining his image???? HAHAHA—-what do you think he did for mine all these years???? (Continues to laugh until she snorts)

So now what? Here I sit at 51 and soon the kid will be on his own...so what now? It strikes me that I don't even know who I am without having to be concerned about the boy 24/7— I support him moving, I was on my own at an early age too—-so I get that. It's just that a moment will catch me and I am like completely undone for a flash. Composure is regained and I keep moving...I am not sure how I will sleep at night not knowing exactly where he is or if he got home safe from work...and I can't always be asking...he will just say I am being a "helicopter parent".

I don't think regular people GET what it is

THE WORKING
WARRIOR MOM

like to give up everything to pour yourself into the job of raising a child ALL on your own and having to pay for EVERYTHING and then all of a sudden it is complete...at least this phase because of course we are always their parents....that is a lifetime position....lucky us:)

Then there is the whole 51 issue...damn if I had $5.00 for every lesson I have learned...honestly it seems like the first 50 years was just training ground...sometimes I wonder how the hell I made it!! Also what is with the lines in my face all of a sudden??? Like where the F did those even come from??? UGH!

So let's talk about some of the "biggies"—lesson wise that is—

- I learned to watch for behavior patterns as well as actions...words I have discovered mean little....actions are important and patterns will tell you even more. Patterns show the history of someone's behavior and that is SO important.

- I learned how to walk through fire and hell and come out the other side and I learned that the fire refines me every time and every time I come out stronger and wiser. The fire seasons are hard, yet they are the biggest gifts. Truly. When you are IN them, they are hellish—-when you are out the other side you come to appreciate their value to your growth.

- I have learned patience...mostly...:)

- I have learned how to set boundaries and how to say NO

- I have learned that I cannot fix people and I cannot save them....no matter how much I love them or how much I want to...only they can save themselves.

- I have learned and seen first hand that no matter how long it takes, karma NEVER loses an address.

- I learned that I am not for everyone and that is OK.

- And lastly I learned to understand my worth and to value that...this one took almost the whole 51 years to get...

There are SO many more...however those are the BIG ones, the ones that came as a result of walking through fire seasons. Life really is a work in progress and change is what keeps pushing us forward...the kid moving will be its own season for me, not quite a fire

THE WORKING WARRIOR MOM

season yet some sort of reclaiming...

Reclaiming parts of myself that I had to put aside in order to effectively be his mother and make it work...it will be interesting to see who I become now that I can breathe a little...I look forward to sharing this coming season with you.

I will say that I am grateful for ALL of what came before and that I have also learned to have GRACE for myself and for others as well as I learned that everything really IS working together for good even when I cannot see.

Elvis Has Left the Building...

Last Saturday we moved the kiddo to NY where he got his first apartment and will go to school and work and make a life that is separate from mine...after 19 years.

I like the area a lot, it's a good area for a 19 year old to make a life, much more to do than in VT. The drive over is easy, it's only 1.5 hours away and he is doing well and finding his way. He doesn't know anyone there, he just decided that he liked the area, found himself an apartment, had me go over and look at the area and then BOOM...they accepted his application for the apartment on the Tuesday after Memorial Day and he asked me to get him moved that Saturday——so I rented us a Penske truck and away we went.

He is just like me you know...making a decision and then executing it cleanly and concisely...no drama, no bullshit just doing the next thing. He is also like me in that he picked an area that he felt was best for him and then even though he was terrified he just did it anyway. People are telling me how brave he is and how I did such a good job that he was able to go and do this...

And me? I'm over here wandering around

THE WORKING
WARRIOR MOM

my CLEAN and QUIET house wondering what the hell just happened...

I think that I am still digesting the fact that we will never live under the same roof again— some of you likely know what a strange freaking feeling that really is. In some ways single Moms are the only ones that can comprehend this fully because they know what it is like to put your head down and focus on one thing—-the kid—and just keep doing the next thing until one day one level of it is complete.

So I keep asking myself, "NOW WHAT?"—who am I if I am not that, what do I want to do now that I am free to decide??? I have spent 19 years just doing what needed to be done to make sure that this kid had everything that he needed and to make sure that we had enough money to pay the bills etc etc. I just had my head down and I lifted it a bit when he graduated and started working and now I am free to lift it all the way and it's WEIRD. There is no other way to describe it— it isn't bad, it is just weird.

Now what? Now what? Now what? I don't know...I mean of course I have a job and people count on me to do it, so I will keep doing that. Trying to get used to nobody bothering me every second of the day because during this pandemic with his restaurant closed that is what was happening—he was literally driving me mad—s-l-o-w-l-y...

The moving was a blessing to both of us and of course I just want him to be happy and functional (LOL) and a good person and learn how to budget!!! Pretty normal shit.

It is so clean here—as in when I clean something it stays clean—-imagine that!?!? That I will gladly get used to—- we talk daily and he is doing well and I am processing and truly all is well. It is just different...19 years of doing something is a long time.

I got the job done though, of that I am certain—- I am looking forward to seeing what he does now and trying very hard to let him figure shit out while providing support— that is a new concept for the chick that wants to fix and save everyone— I'm learning my way as I go...

Onward —-

Notes, Ideas and Thoughts...

A Lesson in Leadership (again)

We were talking about Leadership on last Saturday morning's Coffee Chat Show, and I was reminding you all that everyone is a leader in SOME way in their lives. As parents we are certainly leaders for our children. Below is one of my pieces on Leadership that was included in a book, it is one of my favorites and I wanted to share it with you again:

Often people think of 'Leadership' as something that comes with privilege, they assume that once a person serves in a leadership capacity, they enjoy a 'charmed' life. They forget that REAL leadership is 'power WITH' not 'power over'.

When a calling has been placed on your life to lead, life itself sets out to equip you for it. This usually involves challenges and circumstances that will bring you to your knees.

When you are in God's leadership training you don't get a manual or a letter in the mail, no email comes and no instruction booklet is available. Life just starts to kick the crap out of you, challenges materialize from all over and you can be sure they will include betrayal and disappointment.

THE WORKING
WARRIOR MOM

Many people 'want' to be leaders; they envision that being a leader is important, filled with glory and has a lot of perks...perhaps they even think that being a leader is where the 'money' is. The truth? Being a leader, is in fact, more difficult than any other task. Being a good or great leader? That requires more work than most people can even fathom.

In order to lead you must be able to follow...happily and humbly. You must be able to take direction and work within someone else's framework even if you think you could do it better. If you can't follow someone else then NOBODY will ever follow you, no matter how amazing you perceive yourself to be. This is an important skill to understand, the act of following happily and humbly. I promise you that every great leader began by following someone else first.

To lead successfully you lead by example, you first do the task that you wish to entrust to someone else. You need to have executed that task with excellence to understand what it feels like to complete that particular thing successfully. If you want to direct people then you have to be coming from a place that includes already doing that work, otherwise people will ignore your requests and resent you. If you think you are too good to clean windows or toilets or empty trash, yet you imagine that someone 'beneath' you should do those things, then you are not leadership material. Any attitude of 'entitlement' has no place in leadership.

I don't care who you are or who you think you are—nobody is beneath you and you are not better than anyone else on the planet. You may be different and you may have more advanced skills and you may make more money, however you are not 'better' than any other human being. God created all of us equal and to be a great leader you will do well to remember this and to treat people accordingly.

Real leaders want to build people up and help them get to the next level in their lives; leaders know that their job is to leave everything better than they found it. They make it their business to INSPIRE other people and contribute to them. Leaders speak about possibility, and they refrain from criticism and sarcasm.

There are so many people trying to succeed and lead and they keep forgetting the source of true leadership which is to lead by example. You first must FOLLOW the disciplines that you wish to teach, you must walk the walk and succeed there before anyone will listen to you. Sure, you can lead without doing this and whatever you are trying to do will fall apart, eventually it will collapse on top of you and you won't prosper to your full ability.

You can't sleep late, live like a slob, be rude, and treat people poorly, lack self-discipline and then get dressed up in a suit and go tell people how to be a success. People may look like they are listening, yet you will lack the authenticity needed to produce results. You can put lipstick on a pig, but it is still a pig.

Gandhi said *"Be the change in the world that you want to see"*. Sometimes leaders think that they are an exception to this...

Be authentic, don't try to teach what you haven't learned.

Revealing Leaders

It's early June of 2022 and I am wrapping up this volume of the Practical Change series, thinking about what I want to leave you with…

You have more to contribute, I think it's high time to stop playing small in your life—time to start revealing the leader lurking under the surface.

Everyone has a leader in them hiding out somewhere, waiting for the opportunity to reveal themselves. At the very least you are the leader of your own life and for a time (if you are a parent) the leader of your children's lives. People are often waiting for someone to "do something" about something. Maybe YOU are the someone, maybe it's YOU that the world is waiting for. Perhaps it's time for you to start revealing the amazing qualities that exist only in you, revealing them so that they can contribute to someone else.

One committed person can bring about incredible results if they are willing to take the risk and step out of their comfort zone to do the things that need to be done.

All the power to change your life lives within you. You must be willing to do the

THE WORKING
WARRIOR MOM

work, you have to go to war with the parts of yourself that hold you back, you have to be willing to have a future unlike the past and you have to be willing to let go of your old conversations and stories –the ones that aren't serving you anymore.

What are you telling yourself every day?

What old conversations and stories are you still living in as if they were the truth about you?

Who do you believe you are?

Leading ourselves is a most difficult task because we have to dig out all the things that aren't working and clean them up. If you want a different future, you have to be a different person and in order for that to happen you have to release old versions of yourself.

You know the saying, "what got you here won't get you there".

Complaining breeds complacency and honesty pushes for action.

Brene Brown says, "clear is kind". Be clear with yourself about what isn't working, start telling yourself the truth. Don't fool yourself with your excuses anymore, recognize that the changes you aren't getting are a result of the WORK YOU ARE NOT DOING.

Stop complaining, stop blaming – if you don't have the results you want, what are you willing to DO about it????

You are more of a leader than you imagine, and you have skill sets and qualities that you are not accessing. Maybe you're waiting for the right time to lead, maybe you're waiting for someone to ask you—in which case, consider this as me asking you to step up and lead yourself into the life you want instead of the one you are settling for.

Today is the perfect day to start something new. The time is now and the future you is calling.

Will you answer?

THE WORKING
WARRIOR MOM

With Great Gratitude, I acknowledge and thank the following people...

• My husband John, for his love, care, generosity, determination, incredible personality and for being my rock and for always praying for me and with me. XOXO

• My son, Antonio (boy) for making me laugh, supporting me and inspiring me. I love you to the moon and back.

• MB for holding me up when I could barely hold on, for seeing what I couldn't see all the times that he has, for trusting me, loving me and for always making me better—even when I use too many words.

• Bryan for his friendship, his generosity, his vision and for trusting me with all the "things".

• My Main Prayer Warrior and lifetime companions... Rodney, Tracy, Debi and Miranda... without you I would not be able to do any of this. I love you more.

• Steve O for all the things in all the ways... XOXO

• My badass girl gang...the bestest forever friends...Keely, Stacey, Karen, Kim, Pam, Selena, Jean and Paula. I love you all so much.

- The teams at Delta Hire and Bryn Law Group—you all make my days brighter. Thank you for your hard work, your help, your dedication, and your laughter. You all have my heart.

- SPJ—no words are needed, the cross never comes off, that says it all. XOXOXO

- The Coppola clan for welcoming me into your world with love and grace—I love you all more than words can say.

- Kim, Drew, Michael, Sedrik and Pam thank you for always jumping on board with whatever book or project I throw at you. Your support and assistance are invaluable to me, and I am so grateful for all of you.

- For all friends, clients, and family near and far, thank you for being part of my life.

- The followers and supporters of @wrkingwarriormom and @revealingleaders...thank you for giving me a reason to keep on even when I'd rather not... I love you.

THE WORKING
WARRIOR MOM

About the Author

Noelle Federico is a Master Professional Certified Coach and a results strategist. She is the founder of Fortunato Partners, Inc., a boutique leadership development & consulting firm. Noelle has over three decades of Executive experience across several different industries and has worked in numerous roles within corporate finance, operations, and communications.

Additionally, she serves as the Director of Project Management for BRYN LAW GROUP in Miami, FL as well as the CEO of Delta Hire LLC a national recruiting and workforce development company also based out of Miami. She is a social media influencer, host of THE COFFEE CHAT SHOW and creator of The Working Warrior Mom and The Working Single Mom brands which have a reach of over 2.2 million people monthly. Additionally, she writes, does leadership development, speaks, and consults.

Formerly she spent 14 years, as CFO, CMO and Business Manager of Dreamstime.com LLC, where she was a member of the founding team that created the privately held global stock photography leader.
Her focus has now returned to business management, consulting, and leadership training. In 2009, she founded the TN & VT based non-profit, A Generous Heart, Inc. which runs the Revealing Leaders Program as well as sup-

 THE WORKING WARRIOR MOM

My View from Here...

ports/creates local young literacy programs in partnership with community libraries.

Noelle graduated from Fisher College in Boston, MA and has also attended classes at Suffolk University as well as she holds certificates from Harvard Business School Online in Negotiation Mastery, Entrepreneurial Essentials, Organizational Leadership, Management Essentials, and a Certificate of Specialization in Leadership & Management.

She is a graduate of the Dale Carnegie Training, a Certified Everything DiSC Practitioner and a Landmark Worldwide graduate. Formerly of Boston/ Cape Cod, MA and Franklin, TN …she now resides in Vermont with her husband
John, two large cats, and one small cat named Merlin.

Please visit her at:

www.theworkingwarriormom.com
and
www.revealingexcellence.com

THE WORKING
WARRIOR MOM